EMMANUEL JOSEPH

Decentralized Relief, How Cryptocurrency is Transforming International Aid Missions

Copyright © 2025 by Emmanuel Joseph

All rights reserved. No part of this publication may be reproduced, stored or transmitted in any form or by any means, electronic, mechanical, photocopying, recording, scanning, or otherwise without written permission from the publisher. It is illegal to copy this book, post it to a website, or distribute it by any other means without permission.

First edition

This book was professionally typeset on Reedsy.
Find out more at reedsy.com

Contents

1	Chapter 1	1
2	Chapter 1: The Crisis of Traditional Aid	3
3	Chapter 2: The Birth of a New System	5
4	Chapter 3: Breaking Down Barriers	6
5	Chapter 4: Transparency and Accountability	7
6	Chapter 5: Empowering Local Communities	8
7	Chapter 6: Overcoming Challenges	9
8	Chapter 7: Case Studies in Action	10
9	Chapter 8: The Role of Technology	11
10	Chapter 9: Building Trust with Donors	12
11	Chapter 10: The Future of Decentralized Relief	13
12	Chapter 11: Ethical Considerations	14
13	Chapter 12: A Call to Action	15
14	Chapter 13: Bridging the Digital Divide	16
15	Chapter 14: The Role of Governments and Policy Makers	17
16	Chapter 15: A Vision for Global Equity	18

1

Chapter 1

Introduction: The Dawn of a New Era in Humanitarian Aid

In a world where crises seem to multiply by the day—natural disasters, armed conflicts, pandemics, and economic collapses—the need for effective and timely humanitarian aid has never been greater. For decades, traditional aid systems have been the backbone of global relief efforts, delivering food, medicine, and resources to those in desperate need. Yet, these systems are far from perfect. Bureaucratic inefficiencies, corruption, and logistical hurdles often delay or derail aid, leaving millions vulnerable. In the face of these challenges, a new solution has emerged from an unlikely source: cryptocurrency. What began as a financial experiment has evolved into a powerful tool for transforming how the world delivers aid.

Cryptocurrency, with its decentralized and transparent nature, offers a radical departure from traditional aid models. Built on blockchain technology, it enables secure, real-time transactions that can be tracked by anyone, anywhere. This transparency ensures that funds reach their intended recipients without being siphoned off by intermediaries or corrupt officials. For donors, this means greater confidence that their contributions are making a real impact. For aid organizations, it means the ability to operate more efficiently and effectively in even the most challenging environments. The potential of cryptocurrency to revolutionize international aid is not just theoretical—it is already being put into practice in some of the world's most crisis-stricken regions.

Consider the story of a Syrian refugee family in Jordan, struggling to rebuild their lives after fleeing war. Through a pilot program by the United Nations World Food Programme, they received cryptocurrency-based cash assistance, allowing them to purchase food directly from local markets. This approach not only provided immediate relief but also empowered the family to make their own choices, fostering dignity and self-reliance. Stories like this are becoming more common as aid organizations experiment with decentralized systems, proving that cryptocurrency is more than just a buzzword—it is a lifeline for those in need.

Yet, the adoption of cryptocurrency in humanitarian aid is not without its challenges. Many people, including aid workers and recipients, are unfamiliar with digital currencies. The volatility of cryptocurrencies like Bitcoin can pose risks, and the lack of infrastructure in remote areas can hinder their use. Additionally, regulatory uncertainties and ethical concerns must be addressed to ensure that this technology is used responsibly. Despite these obstacles, the benefits of cryptocurrency—speed, transparency, and accessibility—are too significant to ignore. As the world grapples with increasingly complex crises, the need for innovative solutions has never been more urgent.

This book, *Decentralized Relief: How Cryptocurrency is Transforming International Aid Missions*, explores the intersection of technology and humanitarianism. It delves into the successes, challenges, and future potential of cryptocurrency in aid delivery, offering a comprehensive look at how this groundbreaking technology is reshaping the way we respond to global crises. From empowering local communities to building trust with donors, cryptocurrency is paving the way for a more equitable and efficient aid system. As we stand on the brink of a new era in humanitarian relief, one thing is clear: the future of aid is decentralized, and it starts here.

2

Chapter 1: The Crisis of Traditional Aid

In a world plagued by natural disasters, wars, and pandemics, international aid has long been the lifeline for millions. Yet, traditional aid systems are riddled with inefficiencies. Bureaucratic red tape often delays the delivery of essential supplies, while corruption siphons off funds meant for the most vulnerable. Aid organizations struggle to navigate complex political landscapes, and donor fatigue sets in as people lose trust in where their money goes. The need for a more transparent, efficient, and direct system has never been more urgent. Enter cryptocurrency, a technology that promises to revolutionize how aid is delivered.

Cryptocurrency, with its decentralized nature, offers a way to bypass intermediaries. By using blockchain technology, transactions can be tracked in real-time, ensuring that funds reach their intended destinations. This transparency builds trust among donors, who can see exactly how their contributions are being used. Moreover, cryptocurrencies like Bitcoin and Ethereum operate on a global scale, This chapter sets the stage for understanding how decentralized systems can address the shortcomings of traditional aid.

However, the adoption of cryptocurrency in aid missions is not without challenges. Many aid workers and recipients are unfamiliar with digital currencies, and the volatility of cryptocurrencies can pose risks. Despite these hurdles, the potential benefits are too significant to ignore. This book explores how cryptocurrency is already making a difference in international aid and how it could shape the future of humanitarian efforts.

3

Chapter 2: The Birth of a New System

The concept of decentralized finance (DeFi) emerged as a response to the flaws in traditional financial systems. Cryptocurrencies were initially seen as a tool for financial independence, but their potential for social impact quickly became apparent. Early adopters in the aid sector began experimenting with blockchain technology to create more efficient and transparent systems. These pioneers laid the groundwork for what would become a transformative movement in international aid.

One of the first major successes came in 2017, when the United Nations World Food Programme (WFP) launched a pilot project in Jordan. Using Ethereum-based blockchain technology, the WFP provided cash assistance to Syrian refugees. The program allowed refugees to purchase food directly from local markets, empowering them while stimulating the local economy. This initiative demonstrated the practicality of cryptocurrency in aid missions and inspired other organizations to explore similar solutions.

The rise of decentralized systems also coincided with a growing distrust of centralized institutions. Scandals involving mismanagement of aid funds further eroded public confidence. Cryptocurrency offered a way to rebuild that trust by providing a transparent and immutable record of transactions. This chapter delves into the early experiments that paved the way for the integration of cryptocurrency into international aid.

4

Chapter 3: Breaking Down Barriers

One of the most significant advantages of cryptocurrency in aid missions is its ability to overcome geographical and political barriers. Traditional banking systems often exclude people in crisis zones, leaving them without access to financial resources. Cryptocurrency, however, can be accessed with just a smartphone and an internet connection, making it an ideal solution for remote and underserved populations.

In countries with unstable currencies or hyperinflation, cryptocurrency provides a stable alternative. For example, in Venezuela, where the bolivar has lost much of its value, Bitcoin has become a lifeline for many citizens. Aid organizations have leveraged this trend by distributing cryptocurrency to Venezuelans, enabling them to purchase essential goods and services. This approach not only addresses immediate needs but also empowers individuals to take control of their financial futures.

Moreover, cryptocurrency can bypass sanctions and restrictions imposed by governments. In conflict zones, where traditional aid delivery is often blocked, digital currencies offer a way to provide assistance without relying on local authorities. This chapter explores how cryptocurrency is breaking down barriers and reaching those who need help the most.

5

Chapter 4: Transparency and Accountability

Transparency is a cornerstone of effective aid delivery, yet it has long been a challenge for traditional systems. Donors often have no way of knowing how their contributions are being used, leading to skepticism and reduced funding. Cryptocurrency, with its blockchain technology, provides a solution to this problem by creating a public ledger of all transactions.

Every transaction made with cryptocurrency is recorded on the blockchain, making it impossible to alter or hide. This level of transparency ensures that funds are used as intended and reduces the risk of corruption. Aid organizations can use this feature to build trust with donors, providing them with real-time updates on how their money is being spent.

Accountability is another critical aspect of cryptocurrency in aid missions. By using smart contracts, organizations can set specific conditions for the release of funds. For example, funds could be released only when certain milestones are met, such as the delivery of food or the completion of a medical clinic. This chapter examines how cryptocurrency is enhancing transparency and accountability in international aid.

6

Chapter 5: Empowering Local Communities

Cryptocurrency is not just a tool for delivering aid; it is also a means of empowering local communities. By providing people with access to digital currencies, aid organizations can help them become self-sufficient. This approach shifts the focus from short-term relief to long-term development, creating sustainable solutions to poverty and inequality.

In regions where traditional banking is inaccessible, cryptocurrency can serve as a gateway to financial inclusion. People can use digital wallets to save money, make transactions, and even start small businesses. This financial independence reduces their reliance on aid and fosters economic growth.

Furthermore, cryptocurrency can support local economies by enabling direct transactions between donors and recipients. Instead of relying on intermediaries, funds can be transferred directly to those in need, ensuring that more money reaches the intended beneficiaries. This chapter highlights the transformative potential of cryptocurrency in empowering communities and promoting sustainable development.

Chapter 6: Overcoming Challenges

While the benefits of cryptocurrency in aid missions are clear, there are significant challenges to its widespread adoption. One of the most pressing issues is the lack of infrastructure in many crisis zones. Without reliable internet access or smartphones, people cannot use digital currencies. Aid organizations must work to bridge this digital divide by providing the necessary tools and training.

Another challenge is the volatility of cryptocurrencies. The value of Bitcoin and other digital currencies can fluctuate dramatically, posing risks for both donors and recipients. To address this issue, some organizations are using stablecoins, which are pegged to stable assets like the US dollar. This approach minimizes the risk of volatility while retaining the benefits of blockchain technology.

Regulatory hurdles also pose a challenge. Many governments are wary of cryptocurrency and have imposed restrictions on its use. Aid organizations must navigate these regulations while advocating for policies that support the use of digital currencies in humanitarian efforts. This chapter explores the obstacles to adopting cryptocurrency in aid missions and the strategies for overcoming them.

8

Chapter 7: Case Studies in Action

This chapter delves into real-world examples of cryptocurrency transforming international aid. From the WFP's blockchain-based cash assistance program in Jordan to the use of Bitcoin in Venezuela, these case studies illustrate the practical applications of digital currencies in humanitarian efforts. Each example highlights the unique challenges and successes of integrating cryptocurrency into aid missions.

One notable case is the work of GiveDirectly, a nonprofit organization that uses cryptocurrency to provide direct cash transfers to people in need. By leveraging blockchain technology, GiveDirectly ensures that funds are delivered quickly and transparently. This approach has proven effective in empowering recipients and improving their quality of life.

Another example is the use of cryptocurrency in disaster relief. After the 2020 Beirut explosion, aid organizations used Bitcoin to provide immediate assistance to affected families. The speed and efficiency of cryptocurrency transactions made it possible to deliver aid in a matter of hours, rather than days or weeks. These case studies demonstrate the transformative potential of cryptocurrency in international aid.

9

Chapter 8: The Role of Technology

The success of cryptocurrency in aid missions is closely tied to advancements in technology. Blockchain, the underlying technology behind digital currencies, is constantly evolving. New developments, such as faster transaction speeds and lower fees, are making cryptocurrency more accessible and practical for humanitarian use.

Artificial intelligence (AI) and machine learning are also playing a role in optimizing aid delivery. By analyzing data from blockchain transactions, AI can identify patterns and predict where aid is needed most. This data-driven approach enables organizations to allocate resources more effectively and respond to crises in real-time.

Moreover, the integration of cryptocurrency with other technologies, such as mobile banking and digital identity systems, is creating new opportunities for financial inclusion. This chapter explores the technological innovations that are driving the adoption of cryptocurrency in international aid.

10

Chapter 9: Building Trust with Donors

Trust is essential for the success of any aid organization, and cryptocurrency offers a unique way to build that trust. By providing donors with a transparent and immutable record of transactions, organizations can demonstrate their commitment to accountability. This transparency not only attracts more donors but also encourages them to contribute larger amounts.

Crowdfunding platforms that accept cryptocurrency are also gaining popularity. These platforms allow individuals to support causes they care about directly, without going through traditional intermediaries. The use of blockchain technology ensures that every donation is tracked and accounted for, giving donors peace of mind.

This chapter examines how cryptocurrency is reshaping the relationship between aid organizations and donors, fostering a culture of transparency and trust.

11

Chapter 10: The Future of Decentralized Relief

As cryptocurrency continues to gain traction in the aid sector, its potential for transforming international relief efforts is becoming increasingly clear. The future of decentralized relief lies in the widespread adoption of blockchain technology and the development of new tools and platforms that make cryptocurrency more accessible.

One promising trend is the use of decentralized autonomous organizations (DAOs) in aid missions. DAOs are community-driven organizations that operate on blockchain technology, allowing for decentralized decision-making and resource allocation. This model could revolutionize how aid is delivered, putting power in the hands of local communities.

Another area of growth is the integration of cryptocurrency with other emerging technologies, such as the Internet of Things (IoT) and 5G networks. These advancements could enable real-time monitoring of aid delivery and improve the efficiency of humanitarian efforts. This chapter explores the possibilities for the future of decentralized relief and the role of cryptocurrency in shaping that future.

12

Chapter 11: Ethical Considerations

While cryptocurrency offers many benefits for international aid, it also raises important ethical questions. The anonymity of digital currencies can be both a strength and a weakness. On one hand, it protects the privacy of recipients; on the other hand, it can be exploited for illicit activities.

Aid organizations must also consider the environmental impact of cryptocurrency. The energy consumption required for blockchain transactions has raised concerns about sustainability. To address this issue, some organizations are exploring more energy-efficient alternatives, such as proof-of-stake cryptocurrencies.

This chapter examines the ethical dilemmas associated with using cryptocurrency in aid missions and the steps organizations can take to address them.

13

Chapter 12: A Call to Action

The integration of cryptocurrency into international aid is still in its early stages, but the potential for transformative impact is undeniable. This final chapter calls on aid organizations, governments, and individuals to embrace decentralized systems and support the use of cryptocurrency in humanitarian efforts.

By working together to overcome challenges and build a more transparent and efficient aid system, we can ensure that help reaches those who need it most. Cryptocurrency is not just a technological innovation; it is a tool for creating a more equitable and compassionate world. This book concludes with a vision for the future of decentralized relief and a call to action for all those committed to making a difference.

14

Chapter 13: Bridging the Digital Divide

One of the most significant barriers to the widespread adoption of cryptocurrency in aid missions is the digital divide. In many crisis zones, access to technology is limited, and communities lack the infrastructure needed to use digital currencies effectively. This chapter explores the innovative solutions being developed to bridge this gap and ensure that no one is left behind in the decentralized revolution.

Organizations are partnering with tech companies to provide affordable smartphones and internet access to underserved populations. In refugee camps, for example, solar-powered charging stations and Wi-Fi hubs are being installed to enable connectivity. Training programs are also being rolled out to teach people how to use digital wallets and navigate blockchain-based systems. These efforts are not just about providing tools—they're about empowering communities to take control of their financial futures.

The chapter also highlights the role of local partnerships in overcoming the digital divide. By working with grassroots organizations and community leaders, aid groups can tailor their solutions to the specific needs of each region. This collaborative approach ensures that technology is not imposed from the outside but integrated in a way that respects and enhances local cultures and practices.

15

Chapter 14: The Role of Governments and Policy Makers

As cryptocurrency gains traction in the aid sector, governments and policy makers play a crucial role in shaping its future. This chapter examines the complex relationship between decentralized systems and regulatory frameworks, exploring how governments can support—or hinder—the use of cryptocurrency in humanitarian efforts.

Some countries have embraced cryptocurrency, recognizing its potential to improve aid delivery and financial inclusion. Others have imposed strict regulations, citing concerns about volatility, security, and illicit activities. This chapter delves into the debates surrounding these policies and the need for a balanced approach that fosters innovation while protecting vulnerable populations.

It also highlights the importance of international cooperation in creating a regulatory environment that supports decentralized relief. By working together, governments can develop standards and guidelines that ensure the responsible use of cryptocurrency in aid missions. This chapter calls on policy makers to be proactive in shaping the future of humanitarian aid, rather than reacting to the challenges posed by new technologies.

16

Chapter 15: A Vision for Global Equity

The final chapter of *Decentralized Relief* looks beyond the immediate applications of cryptocurrency in aid missions to envision a future of global equity. It argues that decentralized systems have the potential to address not just the symptoms of poverty and inequality but their root causes. By providing people with access to financial resources and empowering them to build their own futures, cryptocurrency can help create a more just and equitable world.

This chapter explores the broader implications of decentralized systems for global development. It discusses how blockchain technology can be used to create transparent and accountable governance structures, reduce corruption, and promote economic growth. It also considers the role of cryptocurrency in addressing systemic issues like climate change and gender inequality, offering a holistic vision for the future of humanitarianism.

The book concludes with a call to action, urging readers to embrace the possibilities of decentralized systems and work together to build a world where everyone has the opportunity to thrive. It's a vision that goes beyond aid—it's a vision for a better future, powered by innovation, compassion, and the belief that technology can be a force for good.

Book Description: Decentralized Relief: How Cryptocurrency is Transforming International Aid Missions

CHAPTER 15: A VISION FOR GLOBAL EQUITY

In a world where crises are becoming more frequent and complex, the traditional systems of delivering humanitarian aid are struggling to keep up. Bureaucratic delays, corruption, and inefficiencies often prevent life-saving resources from reaching those who need them most. But what if there was a way to cut through the red tape, ensure transparency, and deliver aid faster and more effectively? Enter cryptocurrency—a technology that is quietly revolutionizing the way the world responds to disasters and humanitarian crises.

Decentralized Relief: How Cryptocurrency is Transforming International Aid Missions is a groundbreaking exploration of how blockchain technology and digital currencies are reshaping the landscape of international aid. This book takes readers on a journey through the successes, challenges, and untapped potential of cryptocurrency in humanitarian efforts. From empowering refugees in Jordan to providing financial stability in Venezuela, the stories within these pages illustrate the transformative power of decentralized systems.

Written in an engaging and accessible style, this book is not just for tech enthusiasts or financial experts—it's for anyone who cares about making the world a better place. It delves into real-world case studies, showcasing how organizations like the United Nations World Food Programme and GiveDirectly are using cryptocurrency to deliver aid with unprecedented speed and transparency. It also addresses the hurdles that come with this innovation, from regulatory challenges to the digital divide, and offers practical solutions for overcoming them.

At its core, *Decentralized Relief* is a call to action. It challenges readers to rethink how aid is delivered and to embrace the possibilities of technology in creating a more equitable and efficient system. It's a story of hope, innovation, and the power of human ingenuity to solve some of the world's most pressing problems. Whether you're a donor, an aid worker, or simply someone who believes in the potential for change, this book will inspire you to see the future of humanitarian aid in a whole new light.

The future of aid is here, and it's decentralized. This book is your guide to understanding how cryptocurrency is not just transforming international aid missions—it's redefining what's possible in the fight against global suffering